Viva America!

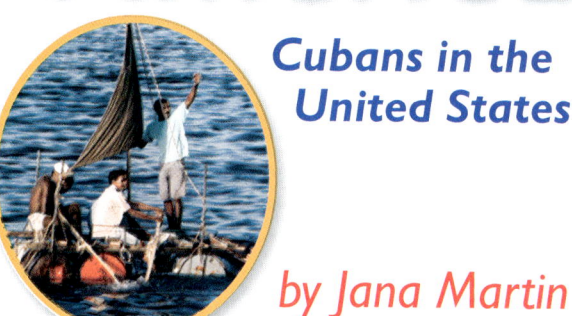

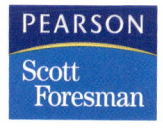

Cubans in the United States

by Jana Martin

PEARSON
Scott Foresman

Editorial Offices: Glenview, Illinois • Parsippany, New Jersey • New York, New York
Sales Offices: Needham, Massachusetts • Duluth, Georgia • Glenview, Illinois
Coppell, Texas • Ontario, California • Mesa, Arizona

Every effort has been made to secure permission and provide appropriate credit for photographic material. The publisher deeply regrets any omission and pledges to correct errors called to its attention in subsequent editions.

Unless otherwise acknowledged, all photographs are the property of Scott Foresman, a division of Pearson Education.

Photo locators denoted as follows: Top (T), Center (C), Bottom (B), Left (L), Right (R), Background (Bkgd)

Opener ©CREUTZMANN SVEN/CORBIS SYGMA; 1 ©Reuters/CORBIS; 3 ©Nik Wheeler/ CORBIS; 5 ©Bettmann/CORBIS; 6(L) ©Bettmann/CORBIS; 6(R) Lake County Museum/ CORBIS; 7(L) ©Bettmann/CORBIS; 7(R) ©Bettmann/CORBIS; 8 ©Bettmann/CORBIS; 9 ©Bettmann/CORBIS; 10 ©Tony Arruza/CORBIS; 12 ©Bettmann/CORBIS; 14 ©Reuters/ CORBIS; 15 ©Reuters/CORBIS; 16(Bkgd) ©Les Stone/CORBIS; 16(B) ©Jeffery Allan Salter/CORBIS SABA; 17 ©CREUTZMANN SVEN/CORBIS SYGMA; 18 ©Morton Beebe/ CORBIS; 20 ©Tony Arruza/CORBIS; p21(T) ©Condé Nast Archive/CORBIS; 21(B) ©Tony Arruza/CORBIS; 22 ©Underwood & Underwood/CORBIS; 22 ©Mitchell Gerber/CORBIS; 23 ©Mitchell Layton/NewSport/Corbis; 23 ©CORBIS SYGMA

ISBN: 0-328-13599-2

Copyright © Pearson Education, Inc.

All Rights Reserved. Printed in the United States of America. This publication is protected by Copyright, and permission should be obtained from the publisher prior to any prohibited reproduction, storage in a retrieval system, or transmission in any form by any means, electronic, mechanical, photocopying, recording, or likewise. For information regarding permission(s), write to: Permissions Department, Scott Foresman, 1900 East Lake Avenue, Glenview, Illinois 60025.

10 11 12 VON4 13 12 11 10

Land of Opportunity

People from all over the world come to the United States in search of a better life. Some want better work opportunities. Some are looking for a place to freely practice their religious or political beliefs.

The Pilgrims were immigrants. In their own homeland, England, they were punished for practicing their religion. So in the early seventeenth century, they came to live in North America.

Immigrants bring their own cultures to their new homes—including religious beliefs, art, music, literature, and dance. They bring their own languages, ways of cooking, and even their own styles of dress. They all have a unique experience when they come to the United States. For one such group, the Cubans, the experience has been especially dramatic. The history of their native country plays a major role in this experience.

An Island in Turmoil

Cuba is an island in the West Indies. It sits just ninety miles south of the state of Florida. The startling changes that the country has undergone since the 1950s have caused thousands of Cubans to leave Cuba for the United States.

Cuba and the United States had close ties in the late nineteenth century. They traded sugar, coffee, and tobacco. Cuban businesses began to set up branches in the United States. The city of Key West, in the southern tip of Florida, is the closest point in the United States to Cuba. It became a new center for Cuban tobacco businesses. Cuban workers traveled freely between Florida and Cuba. Some moved to the United States. They settled in Key West, Tampa, and other cities.

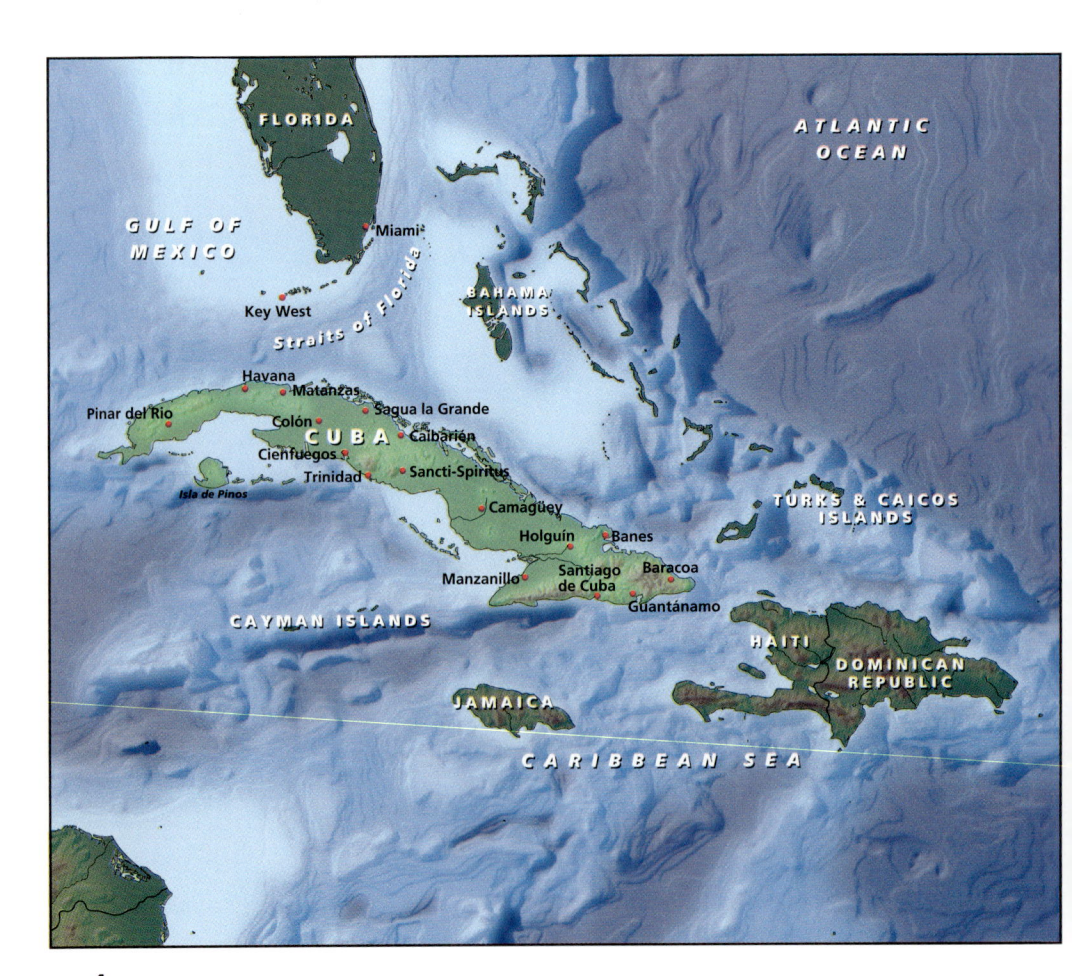

In the 1870s, Cuba itself was in turmoil. The island was under Spanish rule. Spain's policies towards Cubans were harsh, and Spain ignored Cuban **pleas** for fairer treatment. Cubans' attempts to gain independence failed. Some Cubans immigrated to the United States, seeking refuge. Among them was Cuban writer José Martí. He is considered the father of Cuban independence.

Martí was killed when he returned to Cuba to fight for independence. Cuba finally won its freedom in 1898. Spain was defeated in the brief Spanish-American War. A series of Cuban army generals led the nation. The United States maintained a strong interest in Cuba's political and economic affairs.

José Martí

Cuba became a popular **destination** for tourists. From the United States, it was an easy trip. In the capital city of Havana, the hotels were fancy, the restaurants were lively, and the nightlife was unforgettable. In clubs like the Tropicana, talented musicians and dancers entertained audiences all night long. Music such as the mambo combined big band jazz with a Cuban beat that made people want to get up and dance.

Some Cuban professionals and businessmen led a good life, enjoying the benefits of success. Members of the government had many advantages in society, but other Cubans were dissatisfied. More trouble lay ahead.

From the 1930s to the 1950s, Havana was a famous tourist spot.

Cuban Army General Fulgencio Batista was in and out of power throughout the 1930s and 1940s. In 1952 he became dictator of Cuba. His government was repressive and corrupt. It ignored the Cuban Constitution, which said that Cubans had essential rights. Many Cubans felt badly treated and wanted to overthrow Batista. One young lawyer, named Fidel Castro, led a disastrous attempt and landed in jail.

In 1955, Castro was freed from prison. This time, he led a successful revolution. He was supported by groups of students, farmers, and workers. Cuba was turned upside down when Castro defeated Batista in 1959.

General Fulgencio Batista

Fidel Castro took power with the hope of some Cubans riding on his shoulders. But other Cubans fled the country after his victory.

Fleeing Castro

Many older immigrants remember the chaos that followed Castro's takeover. He seized private property and businesses. He punished members of the old establishment. His communist government took control of everything, including trade, farming, housing, education, and the arts.

Some Cubans believed that Castro would improve the country. Others watched in horror. Prosperous farmers, businesspeople, and professionals lost their homes and businesses. Former members of Batista's government were terrified of punishment by the new regime. Educators and artists were suddenly unable to work without government interference.

From 1959 to 1962, more than 200,000 Cubans left Cuba for the United States. Most could only take a few clothes and possessions. Because of their former wealth and position in Cuba, they were called the Golden Exiles.

Cuban refugees arrive in Florida in 1960.

The First Wave

Though they had led proud, prosperous lives in Cuba, many of the Golden Exiles had to start over in the United States. To support their families, doctors became parking attendants, and lawyers became dishwashers. They worked hard to make a living, but they **persisted.**

To be *in exile* means to be "prevented from living in your homeland." At first, many exiles were sure they would only stay in the United States a short while. As soon as Castro was overthrown, they would go home. But Castro was not overthrown. Their Cuba was gone.

Miami, 1963

A feeling of loss was etched into the mindset of these Cuban Americans. It influenced their culture, from songs, politics, and art, to everyday conversations. Children were raised on stories of old Cuba. In new cities, communities recreated versions of the Cuba they loved. No one would forget.

Open Doors

In 1962 Castro declared his loyalty to the Soviet Union, of which Russia was the largest member country. The United States severed its ties with Cuba. This was the era of the Cold War between the United States and the Soviet Union. The two nations disagreed about what style of government was best. The Soviet Union was a communist nation, where the government owned everything, and the United States was a democracy, where people own their own property. Much of the world was divided because of this conflict.

The United States opened its doors to Cuban immigrants. It considered them political refugees. In 1962, U. S. President Lyndon Johnson set up "freedom flights" from Cuba. A refugee center in Miami provided immigrants with medical attention and financial help.

The U. S. government even created laws to help Cubans start their new lives. The Cuban Adjustment Act of 1966 allowed Cubans who had lived in the United States for a year and one day to apply for citizenship. Some 123,000 Cuban immigrants became U. S. citizens.

Cuban immigrants helped create Miami's diverse culture.

By 1973, nearly 300,000 Cubans had entered the country. Many still believed the **menacing** Castro would be overthrown. Then, they thought, they would simply go home. Meanwhile, they joined relatives and communities in cities such as Miami, Florida; Union City, New Jersey; and New York City. They began to adapt to American life. But they also held on to their native Cuban culture and identity.

The city of Miami became a major center of Cuban American life. The first wave of immigrants was now well established. They had created businesses and neighborhoods. The businesses opened up **corridors** to the larger community. The neighborhoods provided newcomers with familiar reminders of life in Cuba.

Some older Cuban immigrants now helped the new Cuban immigrants settle into new homes, jobs, and schools. In the tight-knit Cuban American community, helping each other was important.

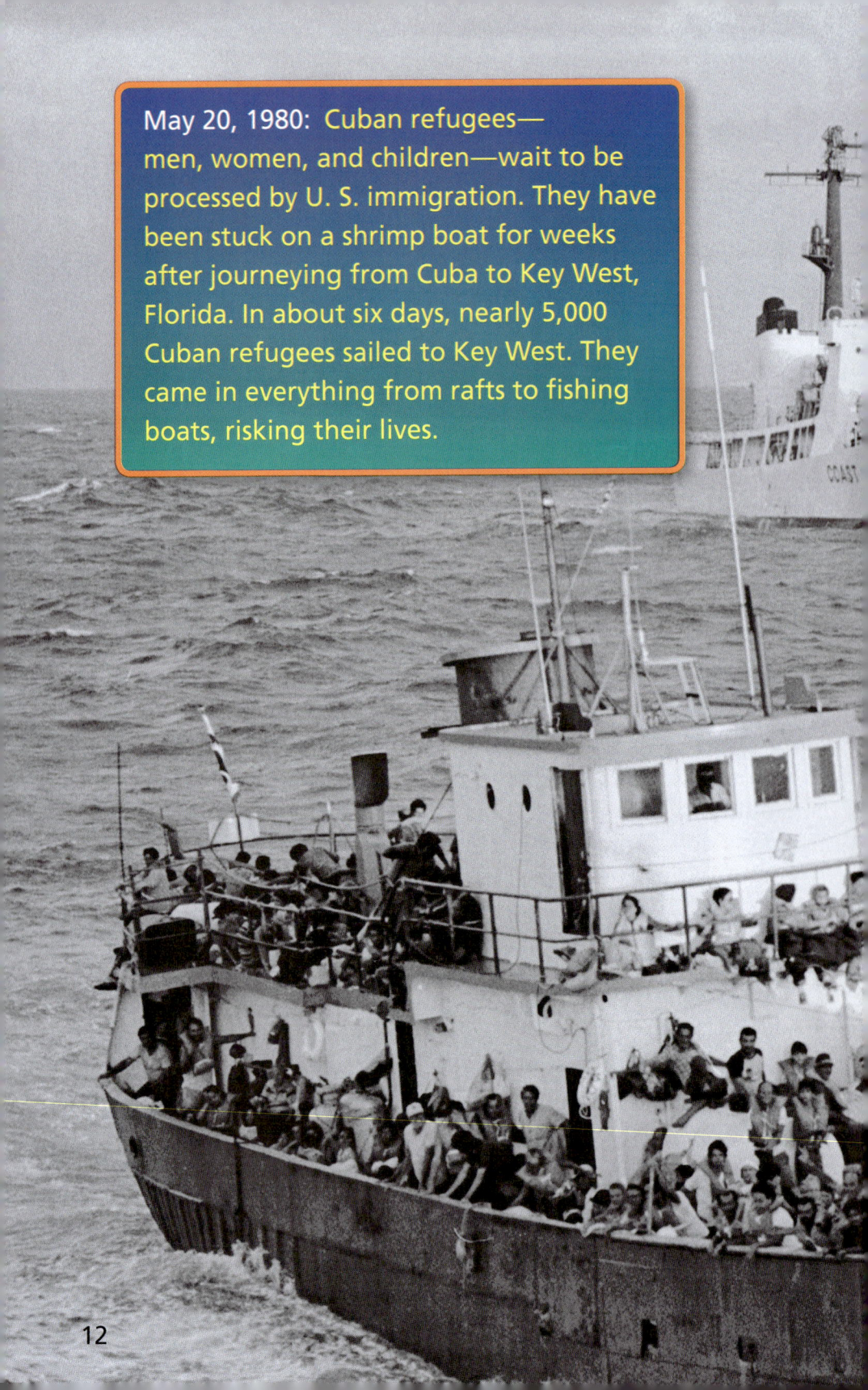

May 20, 1980: Cuban refugees—men, women, and children—wait to be processed by U. S. immigration. They have been stuck on a shrimp boat for weeks after journeying from Cuba to Key West, Florida. In about six days, nearly 5,000 Cuban refugees sailed to Key West. They came in everything from rafts to fishing boats, risking their lives.

Welcome No More

The United States welcomed the first wave of Cuban immigrants. But in twenty years, the story would change drastically.

As many as 700,000 Cubans had already fled their country for a better life. But in 1980, a huge wave of refugees came to the United States. Under international pressure, Castro had opened the port of Mariel. From April to October 1980, 1,700 boats carried 125,000 Cubans to the United States. Nearly all landed in Miami.

The Cubans of the Mariel Boatlift were not well-to-do like the immigrants of the past. Most were poor, looking for a better life. But some were violent criminals who had been released from Cuban jails.

The idea that convicted criminals were about to join U. S. society greatly alarmed the United States. Further, the United States could not process such a huge influx of people so quickly. Instead of helping the new refugees, the U. S. government labeled them undesirable. Instead of support, many *marielitos* received a trip to a detention center. Some stayed there for years.

Former Cuban Air Force Major Orestes Lorenzo Perez defected in 1990 by landing his jet in Key West. For two years, he worked on a plan to reunite his family. On December 19, 1992, Perez flew a small airplane back to Cuba. Lucky enough to escape detection, he landed on a busy street. He picked up his waiting family and returned to Florida.

Cubans continued to immigrate freely to the United States until 1994. That year, the Soviet Union collapsed. Some 50,000 more Cubans fled their country. Many built flimsy rafts out of boards and inner tubes. These people became known as the *balseros*. The journey over open waters was treacherous and dangerous, and many died making the trip. Alarmed, the United States tightened the rules for Cuban immigration. The era of easy entry was over.

Wet Feet, Dry Feet

Today, Cuban refugees are subject to a "wet feet, dry feet" law. In order to be accepted into the United States, a Cuban has to make it onto dry land and have "dry feet." But if a Cuban is still in the water when stopped by the U. S. Coast Guard, and so has "wet feet," he or she is sent back to Cuba.

Just a few more miles —
Cuban rafters head toward U. S. waters.

Cuban American man at an anti-Castro demonstration in New York City

Cuban American teens eating french fries in Fort Lauderdale

To Be Cuban American

What does it mean to be Cuban American? First of all, it means being a refugee of another country. It means speaking Spanish as your first language. In your community, you may speak Spanish; with your friends and even your coworkers, you may speak Spanish. But you still have to adjust to a larger society that speaks English. Some states even have laws prohibiting schools from teaching in Spanish. Although the larger U. S. Latino community increased by 60 percent between 1990 and 2000, there are "English-only" laws in 25 states. Learning a new language takes time, making it harder to start a new life quickly.

Cuban American baseball fans at a U. S.-Cuba game have painted their faces with both countries' flags.

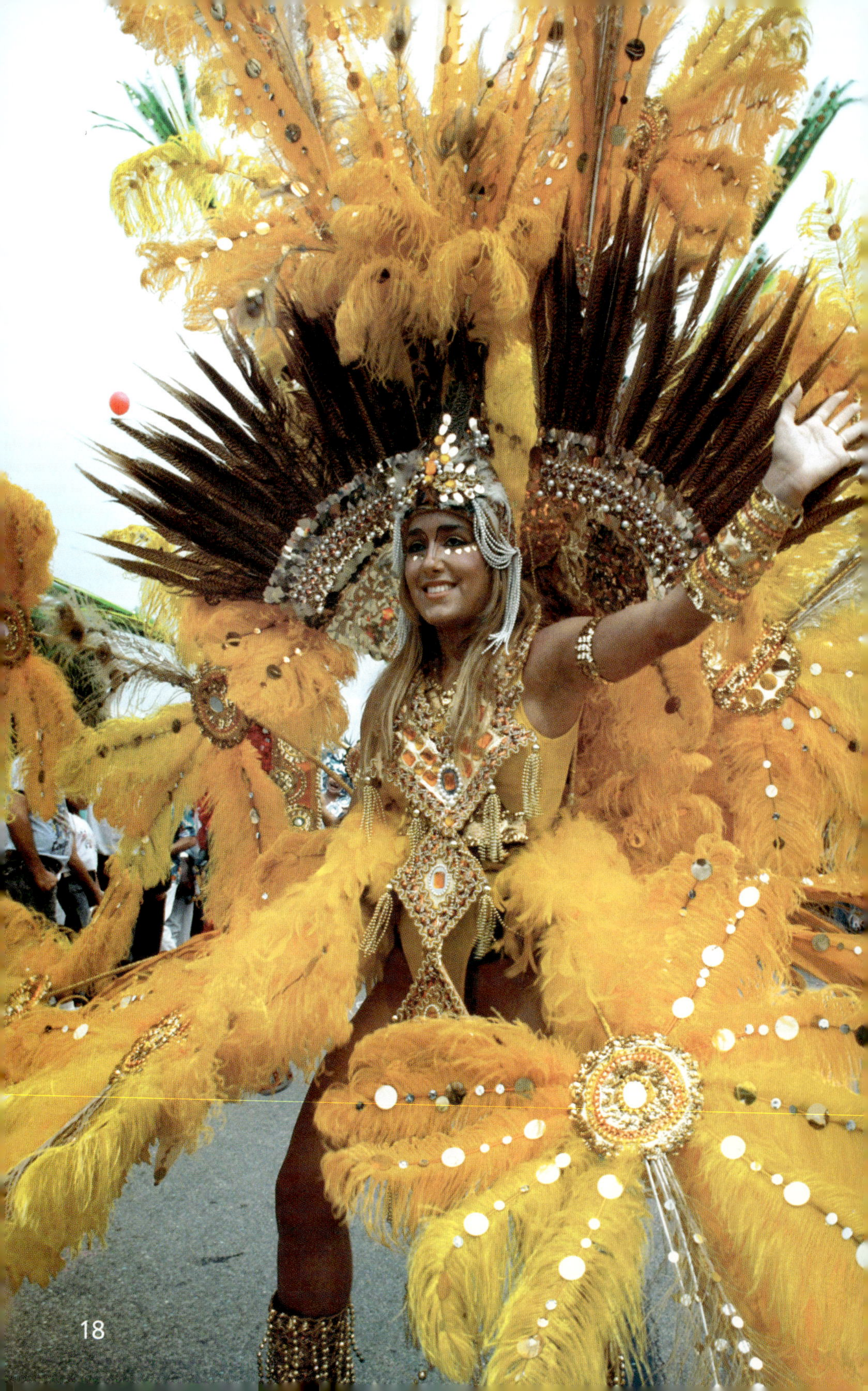

Being a Cuban American may also mean you've left loved ones behind. Many Cuban Americans work hard to send money and supplies back to their families. In other cases, immigrants anger their families by leaving. Sadly, family ties are damaged.

There are now about a million Cuban Americans in the United States—many in Florida, Texas, California, and New York. Everyone has a different story.

The first wave of immigrants—the Golden Exiles—are now the older generation. They are firmly established in their communities. They are professionals, business owners, and politicians. Many remember the upheavals of Castro's revolution. They carry with them this feeling of being forced to leave. Some work hard to try to get Castro out of power. They try their best to strengthen the United States' anti-Castro policy. But their children and grandchildren, who have grown up in the United States, may not feel the same way.

The next waves of immigrants—from the 1960s through to the present—are more diverse. Many have had to struggle to adjust in a less generous climate. Growing up in Castro's Cuba, they may have absorbed a very different way of living. Still, they too are engaged in their communities and in politics. They are artists, professionals, educators, workers, and students. Some are enjoying financial success, while others are still **groping** toward that success.

The *Calle Ocho* (Eighth Street) festival in Miami, Florida, is a huge attraction to people from all over the world. More Cuban Americans live in Miami than any other city in the United States.

19

Cuban store

What holds Cuban Americans together? A strong identity and a unique, vibrant culture. From festivals to food, art, music, dance, language, and literature, they have contributed much to their new home.

Cuban Foods

One way to learn about a culture is through its foods. Cuban food combines Spanish and African traditions with ingredients grown in a tropical climate. Here are some famous Cuban dishes:

- *arroz con pollo*—chicken with yellow rice
- *ropas viejas*—it means "old clothes," but it's really shredded beef
- *platanos maduros*—fried sweet plaintains
- *frijoles negros con arroz*—black beans and rice, served at nearly every meal
- *medianoche*—or "midnight," a pressed, toasted sandwich made with roast pork, ham, and Swiss cheese
- *flan*—a delicious, syrupy, custard dessert
- *batido*—a milkshake made with a tropical fruit such as mango, banana, or papaya and mixed with milk and sugar

Cuban lunch: *batido* and *medianoche*

Family dinner at a Cuban restaurant

21

A Rich Heritage

Cuban Americans include CEOs (chief executive officers) and famous performers. In the 1950s and 1960s, Desi Arnaz became a world-famous bandleader and celebrity. He also costarred in TV's comedy series *I Love Lucy.* Arnaz was the first Latin American to create his own television studio. He also brought Cuban music—from the rumba to the conga—to millions through his shows.

U. S. Secretary of Commerce nominee Carlos Gutierrez came from Cuba in 1960. He was six years old when he and his family fled Cuba. Gutierrez started as a truck driver for a cereal company. Years later he became the company's CEO.

Bandleader and television star Desi Arnaz

Actress Cameron Diaz

Well-known Cuban American actors include Cameron Diaz, whose father is a second generation Cuban-American. Eva Mendes was born in Houston, Texas, and raised in Los Angeles and Miami. Andy Garcia was five years old when his family fled Cuba in 1961. Garcia has talked much of his immigrant experience. He said recently, "I'm Cuban American, and I'm proud of it. I have the benefit of two great cultures." But he added, "You are always at a loss for the one thing you most cherish—the country you were born in."

Summary

Cuban Americans immigrated to the United States in several waves. The first was well received. But by the late 1990s, the United States changed its open-door policy. It became harder to come to the United States. Still, Cubans have created strong communities, such as the one in Miami. They are bound by a rich culture, a common language, and a desire to help each other. They also share the experience of having lost one home and found another.

Jose Contreras was on the Cuban national baseball team before immigrating to the United States in 2003. He has pitched for the New York Yankees and the Chicago White Sox.

Actor Andy Garcia

Glossary

corridors *n.* narrow hallways

destination *n.* the place where one is going

groping *v.* searching blindly or uncertainly

menacing *adj.* threatening

persisted *v.* repeatedly tried to achieve a goal

pleas *n.* desperate requests; cries